Dinner Party Disasters

Dinner Party Disasters

True Stories of Culinary Catastrophe

By Annaliese Soros

With Abigail Stokes

Illustrations by Roderick Mills

ABRAMS IMAGE

NEW YORK

Menu

INTRODUCTION

The idea for this book came to me after many, many years of hosting (and attending) small, intimate dinners, cocktail parties of all sizes, and large fundraising events. What better way to eliminate the fear of hosting than to have some of the most intrepid hosts and hostesses I know share their worst nightmares? This book is proof that, at least for all things culinary, every cloud has a silver lining.

My first real dinner party disaster occurred soon after I began to entertain as a young newlywed. My then-husband, the financier George Soros, and I had rented a house for the summer in Sagaponack, on the south shore of Long Island, New York. We invited about twenty-five people for cocktails and a buffet-style dinner. I made a delicious lamb stew with spring vegetables, a mixed green salad, a platter of assorted cheeses with baguettes, and for dessert, apple strudel. My stove in the rented house was electric, which I wasn't used to, and I burned the stew. Cursing the real estate gods and Thomas Edison, I was ready to send everyone home before a fast-thinking friend said, "Just serve the stew and leave everything to me." He then proceeded to walk around the dinner party from group to group announcing, with brazen confidence, "Isn't it amazing what

6

tarragon can do?" Ironically there was no tarragon in the stew, but because of his ingenuity nobody seemed to notice that the stew was burnt. People even called me the next day to thank me and ask for my tarragon lamb recipe!

I grew up in a small village in northern Germany (population 800), across the road from my grandparents' farm, Dierksin-Hof. At an early age I developed an affinity for good food, simply prepared. During and after the Second World War especially, I came to appreciate how fortunate we were to always have enough—many in Europe at the time went hungry—and doubly, that it was so fresh, coming almost directly from the earth to our table. My mother and my Aunt Anna were excellent cooks who always produced satisfying meals with whatever was in season: venison in a good cream sauce, beef rouladen, or roasted pork. When meat was scarce, we ate root vegetables and potatoes, creamy turnip soup, or perfectly crisp potato pancakes. Cooking was planned around the harvest or the hunt, or the biggest event every year—the slaughtering of a pig. This was such a big event that my mother always confused the date with my birthday! Fortunately, my pragmatic outlook on life spared me years of therapy.

Aunt Anna and her husband owned a bakery in town, so we always had good breads—fresh rolls, rye, pumpernickel—

and even cakes. Sweets, especially chocolate, were scarce after the war, which probably accounts for my lifelong addiction to this confection. It also explains why I seldom fail to serve dessert at a dinner party and always keep ice cream, cookies, and brownies stocked in my freezer.

At twenty-one I decided to see the world and immigrated to New York as an au pair on Long Island. In 1960, I married George, whom I had met at a weekend house in Quogue, Long Island, in 1957. During our first year of marriage, we both enjoyed an eight-course dinner thrown by a Brazilian friend, which she somehow produced out of a kitchen the size of a broom closet. That got my competitive juices flowing, so I went out and bought various cookbooks. Eventually, *Michael Field's Cooking School* and then *Mastering the Art of French Cooking* by Julia Child became my bibles. Now my cookbook library includes a bound collection of my own family recipes, the Silver Palate books, the Barefoot Contessa books, and the early Martha Stewart books, among many others.

George and I built a house in Southampton (near the scene of my first disaster), and we had guests nearly every weekend. That really sharpened my cooking and entertaining skills. Over the years, I improved with trial and error (for example, I learned the hard way that ricotta will not do in tiramisu when mascarpone is unavailable). It is a method I really only recommend for meals with family and close friends. However, most of my efforts were very successful, a conclusion I reach in part because George wanted to come home for lunch even during the business week.

These days, if I'm going to entertain on the weekend, I sit down with my cookbooks by Wednesday and plan the menu. I always look for new ideas in the Food section of *The New York Times* and on various cooking shows on PBS, and I follow the "in" chefs to see whether I can borrow any ideas from them. Some years ago, I actually began keeping a record in a binder of who ate what and when, and I plan the menu accordingly. I suppose I should ask guests about allergies, but somehow, that has never been a problem. And I can't possibly keep track of what diet is in vogue. In any case, it always seems to be the people on diets who forget their self-discipline after arriving at my house.

I shop for groceries on Thursday and Friday, and begin work in the kitchen early on Saturday. Preparation is the most important ally in the war against catastrophe.

I still host large parties—as many as fifty for a seated dinner—but a more typical number is twelve. I enjoy being able to talk with all of my guests, so I now often enlist the aid of a caterer. I try to keep the dinners low-key and intimate, yet lively. I find having a theme is helpful. Holidays and birthdays are the obvious ones; since I have an abiding interest in music, musicales are both pleasurable and practical, as they give an evening a focal point. For one particularly memorable dinner party, I hired a magician, who "stole" (and returned) the wallets and watches of my guests!

I don't always have music playing, but a stack of CDs is at the ready in case a void needs to be filled. Classical music is my passion, which may not appeal to everyone, but to me it is the least obtrusive. Usually I choose pieces written for chambers or living rooms—Mozart, Vivaldi, or Haydn—nothing with vocals, as they are a distraction from the conversation, which is kept flowing with plenty of good wine and spirits.

I try to invite people whom I think have something in common. Then I can be fairly certain they'll find something to talk about, though I don't believe in feeding the conversation. I try to mix singles and couples—if people only thought in terms of couples, I would never be invited to a dinner party! (George and I were divorced in 1983.) While I'm rather laissez-faire about the conversation, I'm not so about the seating: I usually assign seats based on common interests, aiming to alternate men and women. I avoid putting husbands and wives next to each other.

In spite of my best efforts to put together people who share similar, or at least complementary, interests, there are the inevitable gaffes. I remember an incident involving a friend who was highly intelligent and—usually—quite entertaining. When inspired, he could command the table with riveting stories and effortless wit. He was seated next to an outgoing and rather chatty woman, who asked him how life was in the former Yugoslavia, where he was from. "I don't give a f—k about Yugoslavia," he shouted at her. She did not say much after that but appeared immensely interested in her soup. What can you do? After that incident, I invited my friend only to events where the other guests were already familiar with him, or had very thick hides.

I know people for whom conversation is second nature—it flows out of them so naturally and effortlessly, they could talk to anyone, from the meekest wallflower to the most headstrong person in the room. I highly recommend cushioning your guest list with one or two people like this, as they make hosting a party so much easier. For me, these are my children, who on top of their conversational skills, are appreciative and gracious guests.

In case things do go wrong during the cooking, or if guests drop in unexpectedly, I keep the larder stocked with my own version of "emergency rations" (see "The Anti-Catastrophe Pantry," page 92). I always have fruit and sweets on hand for snacks or quick desserts, and as much wine as my wine rack will hold. I'm a strong believer that a great wine is wasted on a bad meal—but by the same token, it's a shame not to complement well-prepared food and a nice atmosphere with a fine bottle of wine.

This book is not really about disasters, any more than a dinner party is strictly about the food. It's about solutions, grace under pressure, and the transitory, human aspects of entertaining with food—the communal rite of breaking bread and celebrating the bonds between a group of friends, new or old.

P.S. A rule of thumb for both books and dinner parties: disasters almost always make great stories, whether in the making or in the telling. The most important ingredient in either case is a sense of humor. That's what turns traumas into triumphs.

Dinner Party Disasters

THE TRIBAL HIGHBALL

HOSTS: Alice & John Ford
NUMBER OF GUESTS: 10
MENU: Cocktails, butternut squash soup,
roast duck, frisée salad, selected cheeses,
fall berries and cream

For many years, my husband and I had cherished the friendship of an elderly explorer who had adventured his way through the jungles of Africa and Brazil in the 1920s and 1930s. Through most of his ninety-three years, he had remained a bachelor, but in his late seventies, he succumbed to the charms of a woman, Mrs. X I'll call her, who had many loves—cats, alcohol, and Mr. X among them, though not necessarily in that order.

One autumn evening, we invited the happy couple to join us for cocktails and an intimate dinner. Mrs. X was a practiced and tidy drunk, so it wasn't until well into the entrée that I thought I noticed her slipping in her seat. "I am imagining things," I thought, glancing between my husband and hers for any acknowledgment of the situation. I got none, but I did notice that our lovely, old, fat cat, Bentley, had crawled under the table and was hidden beneath the voluminous tablecloth. Apparently, Mrs. X had also noticed the cat's movements because she proceeded to slide under the table with a grace I would not have imagined possible in an eighty-year-old woman, and began quietly stroking and talking to the purring animal. Soon after, judging by her soft snores, Mrs. X had fallen asleep. What to do?

I thought I could discern curiosity in the expressions of some of the other guests, but it was entirely possible that they were instead reacting to the shrunken heads Mr. X had chosen to extract from a suitcase he'd brought with him to dinner. Mr. X fondly and repeatedly referred to one of them as "Boris," as if, perhaps, he had done the shrinking himself, as a kind gesture. No one mentioned Mrs. X and the cat.

Salads and cheeses consumed, dessert enjoyed, and it was still unacknowledged that we were one absent at the table. "Let's go to the living room for coffee," I suggested, and so we did, leaving the sleeping Mrs. X and the all-too-enchanted Bentley hidden beneath the folds of the tablecloth.

Halfway through the baroque ritual of filling and refilling our demitasse cups of coffee, Mrs. X appeared, looking slightly disheveled but refreshed and with one request, for a highball. "Indeed," thought I, and handed her one with glee.

Whatever Mr. X had taught us about the mores of the indigenous tribes of Africa and the Amazon, I believe he and Mrs. X had illustrated a variant closer to home: the tribal chic of New York City.

Hangover Management

Alcohol can be a social lubricant that is justifiably credited with easing the flow of conversation and even occasionally with transforming a dull fête into an electric evening. As a thank you to those who've made the party unforgettable, you might suggest one of these hangover remedies as they stumble out your door. Better yet, have "hangover goodie bags" at the ready for those you think may be in need.

To ease the symptoms of a hangover before bed:

> Two regular or extra-strength aspirin (500–1000 mgs) with a rehydrating sports drink like Gatorade, and one 25 mg Dramamine tablet
>
> One tablet vitamin B-complex
>
> A banana smoothie sweetened with honey (if you can manage)

Upon waking:

> Tomato juice or the timeless Bloody Mary ("hair of the dog")
>
> A hearty breakfast of eggs and lots of carbohydrates
>
> A walk and some fresh air (bring sunglasses!)

Don't forget, there is a fine line between lubricated and looped. Guests who become more entertaining as they slip into the state of drunkenness are the exceptions. More often than not, a drunk in your home is a nuisance—one that cannot always be avoided, but one that can be managed. The first thing to do when guests get too deep into their cups is to make sure they don't drink any more alcohol. Offer a non-alcoholic alternative or, in extreme cases, simply replace their drink without asking. Use stealth if you need to; remember, they are impaired! If they drove, take away their car keys. The only option may be to, Fagin-like, pick their pocket, rather than to actually ask for the keys, and to call a taxi. Call 911 if the situation gets out of control or if the person is in danger of harming himself or others.

In the aftermath, review your invitation list and discern who was naughty and who was nice. Revise accordingly.

BUBBLE BUBBLE

HOSTS: Katherine & Boris Ismay
NUMBER OF GUESTS: 8
MENU: Brazilian stew, green salad

I once almost made the fatal mistake of serving my guests a hearty helping of botulism, a move that would certainly have ended my reputation as a good host.

My soirée for eight was scheduled to begin at 7:30. By mid-afternoon the table was set, the salad made, and the dressing ready to be tossed at the proper time. Also on the menu was a hearty Brazilian stew of hot and sweet sausages, red beans, lime juice, bananas, and peanuts, an oft-made dish at our house. It had been simmering on the stove for several hours. By 4:30, as I turned off the flame, the complex mixture gurgled slowly, like lava cooling.

My fourteen-year-old son, James, arrived home from school around 5:00 with his hungry friend, Daniel, in tow. Daniel, as he was wont to do, edged into the kitchen, removed the heavy orange casserole cover, inhaled the stew's lusty aroma, and turned beseeching eyes in my direction. Having made enough for a crowd, I nodded yes. As Daniel was poised to dip the ladle into the pot, I happened to peek inside. The stew, strangely enough, was still bubbling, although experience told me the surface, by now, should have been calm. In fact, although the aroma was still overpoweringly alluring, the bubble activity had actually increased.

Shuddering, I shoved the spoon away from poor Daniel's mouth, and replaced the cover on the stewpot. A quick check of the unused sausage in the fridge revealed it to be the culprit; it had a telltale overripe, slightly rancid odor. I stuck the evil stew outside our back door, feeling, with relief, like a heroic lifesaver—one who now had to save a dinner party.

Luckily, the hors d'oeuvres were plentiful and not potentially deadly. I ordered in several pizzas to the guests' tastes, and, with the addition of bountiful quantities of salad and wine, we partook of a festive Survivors' Fete rather than a Last Supper.

THE SPOILS OF FOOD—WHEN TO LET IT GO

Fish and houseguests begin to smell after three days, Ben Franklin famously posited—at that stage both should be shown the door. As a rule of thumb, meat, poultry, and fish should be odorless until you've started your cooking magic.

Your refrigerator and freezer must be set at the correct temperature before we can discuss how long food will survive in it. Refrigerator/freezer thermometers (available at housewares and hardware stores) are specially designed to provide accurate readings even at very cold temperatures. Refrigerators should maintain a temperature no higher than 40°F. Frozen food holds its top quality for the longest possible time if the freezer maintains 0°F.

Be sure to note the use-by date on store-bought meat and dairy products. Below is a guide to keep foods from spoiling and safe for consumption:

Product	Refrigerator	Freezer
Ground hamburger, turkey, lamb, veal, pork	1–2 days	3–4 months
Fresh meat, chop or roast	3–5 days	6–9 months
Fresh poultry	1–2 days	9 months
Fresh fish	1–2 days	3–6 months
Uncooked sausage	1–2 days	1–2 months

Product	Refrigerator	Freezer
Bacon	7 days	1 month
Cooked fish, meat, poultry	3–4 days	3–6 months
Eggs in the shell	3 weeks	don't freeze
Raw egg yolks and whites	2–4 days	1 year
Commercial mayonnaise, after opening	2 months	don't freeze
Milk, after opening	7 days	don't freeze

For more information, contact:
USDA Food and Safety Inspection Service, www.fsis.usda.gov/
FDA Food Information Line, 1 (888) SAFEFOOD (toll-free)

Unfortunately there is no help line for overly ripe guests.

A LOBSTER TALE

HOSTS: Ellen & Peter Orford
NUMBER OF GUESTS: 20
MENU: Roasted potatoes, corn-on-the-cob,
baked lobster

Several years ago, when we were all young marrieds, my sister and brother-in-law joined us for a time-share in a beach house in the Hamptons, near New York City. At the time, I was interested in cooking and was working my way through one of the cookbooks of Craig Claiborne, the *New York Times* food critic. I decided my contribution to the weekend would be a totally fabulous clambake, substituting lobster for clams. For authenticity, we would cook them in a pit on the beach, over warm briquettes and covered with damp seaweed.

My sister and I spent an entire day rounding up the necessities: a shovel, charcoal and matches, potatoes, ears of corn, lobsters (note to self: buying live lobsters is not fun, and transporting them is even less fun), and huge trash bags for collecting seaweed (this is also no small feat, given the weight and sliminess of the stuff). But all for the greater good of a fabulous lobsterbake! The men were responsible for beer and wine.

As dusk approached, we dug our pit, threw in the briquettes, lit them, waited for them to cool, then piled on the food. We oh-so-carefully and gently covered the pit with damp seaweed and repaired to our beach blankets to await, with the other ten or so couples, our beach feast to finish baking.

A few bottles of wine later, darkness and hunger pangs had set in. We decided to peek under the seaweed to see how things were cooking. To our utter bewilderment, the lobsters were gone. Those determined little crustaceans had clawed their way out of the pit and were heading as fast as they could back to the ocean! In the darkness, we could just make out their ungainly shapes clambering toward the surf.

The story has a happy ending—if you're a lobster. We let them go. Or rather, they let themselves go. Apparently we had not set up our "oven" correctly, allowing the coals to cool a little too much before piling on the food. The corn and potatoes had not made a break for freedom, but, alas, were inedible. Luckily, the hilarity and booze saved the situation. We cleaned up, headed for the dump, and then on to the local clam shack.

PREVENTION OF CRUELTY TO CRUSTACEANS

The king of crustaceans—the lobster—contains sweet, firm, succulent meat within its claws, tail, and body cavity. Lobsters must be cooked alive or killed immediately before they are cooked. And therein lies the rub…

According to the Lobster Institute at the University of Maine, "The nervous system of a lobster is very simple—not unlike that of an insect. Neither insects nor lobsters have brains. For an organism to perceive pain it must have a more complex nervous system. Neurophysiologists tell us that lobsters, like insects, do not process pain."

Advocates at LobsterLiberation.com disagree: "Like all animals, lobsters can feel pain, and they suffer when they are cut, broiled, or boiled alive. Boiling lobsters alive is illegal in Reggio, Italy. Offenders face fines of up to $600."

If you plan to boil live lobsters, drop them headfirst into boiling water. Some believe the best way to minimize the lobsters' "experience" is to chill them by putting them in the freezer or a bucket of ice water for fifteen minutes before dropping them in water that has come to a rolling boil. If you plan to cook them by another method, such as broiling, they need to be killed first. To kill a lobster quickly and humanely, flatten the lobster on its belly and with one hand grasp the tail where it joins the body. With a sharp knife, stab the head just behind the eyes, forcing the knife through to the cutting board, then pressing it forward to divide the head in two.

Now don't you feel better?

mummified

HOSTS: Violet & Alfred Gérmont
NUMBER OF GUESTS: 2
MENU: Orecchiette with garlic and olive oil,
lamb loin with porcini mushrooms, tiramisu

As a newlywed, I lived with my husband, an Italian, in a palatial but sparsely furnished villa in Florence, Italy. For our first dinner party, I hoped to distract our guests' attention from the lack of furnishing by filling the *salotto* with flowers and candles.

It was late October, so there were masses of white mums for sale at all the neighborhood florists. Relating them to autumn and football, I took advantage of their size and abundance to create a very lush environment. Since we were living across from the Church of Santa Croce, I slipped in and made a generous donation to the nearest saint in order to gather up a large number of the tall thin candles stacked before its image.

Of course, I thought the place looked terrific, and could not understand the surprised and somewhat uncomfortable looks on the faces of our guests. It wasn't until my husband arrived home from work and burst out laughing that we all understood the source of our mutual discomfort. Alfred was well aware of football season in the U.S. and immediately understood why I had been drawn to the mums. He explained this to our Italian guests, who immediately relaxed. Very amused, they explained to me that November fourth is All Saints Day (a close relative of our Halloween), when Italians leave white mums at the graves of their loved ones. Faced with a huge room dimly lit by the glow of church candles and filled with banks of mums on tables, mantles, and in vases, our guests were probably wondering whether they had been invited to a dinner or a wake!

After that experience, I now use pumpkins and gourds when I want a fall-themed dinner décor.

THE LANGUAGE OF FLOWERS

Throughout history, people have given flowers as a token of their longing, gratitude, and good wishes. The gift of flowers is a lovely gesture whether for a birthday, an anniversary, or as a thank you for an enjoyable dinner party. But be sure you are sending the intended message.

Acacia—beauty in retirement

Ambrosia—"your love is returned"

Anemone—sincerity; forsaken love

Aster—symbol of love

Azalea—"take care of yourself"

Bluebell—humility

Cactus—endurance

Caladium—great joy and delight

Camellia—good-luck gift for a man

Chrysanthemum—"you are a wonderful friend"

Crocus—gladness

Daffodil—respect and "the sun always shines when I am with you"

Daisy—loyal love and innocence

Forget-me-not—true love and good memories

Freesia—trust

Honeysuckle—happiness

Hyacinth—"please forgive me"

Hydrangea—"thank you for understanding"

Iris—wisdom, faith, and hope

Jonquil—affirmation of mutual affection
Larkspur—fickleness
Lily of the Valley—beauty, gaiety, coquetry
Magnolia—nobility
Marigold—grief
Narcissus—"stay as sweet as you are"
Orchid—thoughtful, maturity, charm
Petunia—"your presence soothes me"
Primrose—"I cannot be without you"
Stephanotis—happiness in marriage
Sweet Pea—"thanks for a lovely time"
Sunflower—pride, sunshine
Tulip—luck and "you are a perfect lover"
Violet—faithfulness, virtue
Viscaria—"dance with me"
Wisteria—welcome

HOT MEXICAN NIGHTS

HOSTS: Madeleine & Andrew Jordan
NUMBER OF GUESTS: 8
MENU: Shrimp ceviche, chalupas,
arroz rojo, flan

One night when my husband, Andrew, was in his cooking phase, he decided to make something Mexican for a group of our close friends. He settled on chalupas, which needed to be fried in an inch or so of oil. When Andrew finished, he turned off the flame and joined us for pre-dinner drinks. Or so he thought. What he'd actually done was turn up the flame, which eventually ignited the oil. Relaxing with our cocktails in the living room, separated from the kitchen—and the smoke—by a door and eighty feet of hallway, we were oblivious to the grease fire consuming our dinner, not to mention the kitchen.

Suddenly, we heard a furious ringing from both the first floor intercom and the front doorbell. Alarmed, we ran to the door. In stormed four burly firemen in full regalia with axes and hatchets at the ready. When they threw open the kitchen door, billows of black smoke emerged. The firemen quickly got the blaze under control, but the kitchen and dinner were in complete shambles. A neighbor across the way had seen the flames from his window and called 911. I have absolutely no recollection what we did for dinner that night, but I believe we owe our neighbor, and the New York City Fire Department, an invitation for supper—ordered out.

The Basics of Fire Prevention

Most fires start out small, but within minutes, or even seconds, they can get out of control.

Smoke detectors are your first line of defense against fires. Install smoke detectors on every level of your home and outside of sleeping areas. Replace batteries twice a year (to remember, do it when you change your clocks between Standard Time and Daylight Saving Time).

Fire extinguishers remain your best bet if you're on the spot when a small fire begins. It's wise to have a fire extinguisher in the kitchen—ten feet away from the stove on the exit side of the room. Purchase an ABC-type extinguisher that can be used on all types of fires. Aim the extinguisher at the base of the fire and use a sweeping motion. (Firefighters teach the acronym PASS: Pull, Aim, Squeeze, and Sweep.) Use an extinguisher on small fires only. If there is a large fire, get out immediately and call 911 from another location.

Devise an escape strategy and review the plan with all members of your family. Agree on an outside location to gather for a head count. Never go back into a burning building for any reason.

An electrical coil on the stove reaches a temperature of 800ºF. A gas flame reaches temperatures above 1,000º. Your dishtowel or potholder can catch fire at 400º. So can your bathrobe, apron, or loose sleeve—so always wear close-fitting clothing when you cook. Tight clothes can keep those home fires burning *and* help prevent your house from burning down.

Power Play

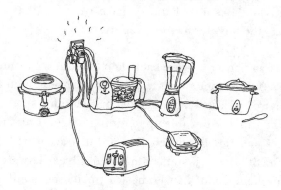

HOSTS: Philippa & Albert Beach
NUMBER OF GUESTS: 2
MENU: Tomato and cucumber salad,
mushrooms on toast, grilled porterhouse
steaks, baked potato, chocolate pots de crèmes

In 1951, I was a working journalist, living at home (as girls did more than fifty years ago), and had just become engaged to be married. My mother, who didn't know where the kitchen was in her own home, thought I should take cooking classes Cordon Bleu. I turned down her suggestion with a rather unbecoming smugness, reminding her that I had received A's in chemistry at Brown University. And anyone who could follow directions for experiments in a university laboratory could certainly follow a recipe in a cookbook. Besides, I didn't have time for that sort of thing—too busy being a girl reporter.

It was also a tradition back then that one's parents were one's first dinner guests. In our small three-room apartment we had a cocktail table that had a hidden spring. That spring flipped the table up to dining height. I never could figure out how it worked, but it did. I set it with Leron linen, Steuben crystal, hammered silver flatware from Shreve and Co. of San Francisco (matching candlesticks, ashtrays, and salt and pepper shakers, of course)—all lovely wedding presents.

There were wedding gifts in the kitchen as well, all being used: there was a handsome wooden, silver-footed salad bowl with silver-handled utensils; an electric toaster for the first course of mushrooms on toast; a large electric something-or-other to bake potatoes; a marvelous huge electric gizmo on which we could make steaks; and a large electric coffeemaker that my office colleagues had given me. I had made the dessert—chocolate pots de crèmes in lovely Limoges cups—the night before, and it was in the fridge chilling.

Mummy and Daddy arrived and were served their favorite cocktails: Bourbon Old Fashioned for her, Scotch Old Fashioned for him. No problem. I'd been making them since I was twelve years old. And so, while they were sipping happily, I went into the kitchen to start dinner.

I plugged in the toaster. I plugged in the potato baker. I plugged in the steak cooker. I plugged in the coffeemaker and—bingo—the entire apartment turned inky black. Yup. I'd really blown it—the fuse, that is—and there were no spares. I lit candles so we could see a little. However, I had never even tried turning on the stove. I didn't know how.

Tomato and cucumber salad and a creamy chocolate dessert isn't a badly balanced meal, is it?

My parents were relieved that I never dared invite them for dinner again.

P.S. I still haven't learned how to cook.

ESSENTIALS OF HOME ELECTRICITY

The basic thing to know about the electrical setup in your home is whether you have a system that relies on fuses or circuit breakers to protect against overheating and fire by interrupting the flow of electricity. Fuses have filaments like lightbulbs that burn out when a circuit is overloaded, breaking the circuit and shutting down any potentially dangerous appliances plugged into it. Fuses have to be replaced, so always keep extras on hand. Circuit breakers are switches that can be flipped on and off. They're easy to switch back on, but you have to know where your circuit box is located and which switch corresponds to each area of your house or apartment. Be sure to unplug the offending appliance before reinstating power.

If a circuit breaker trips frequently, call your electrician to determine what the problem is and fix it. Electrical overloads happen when you have too many appliances on the same line. Every appliance draws a certain amount of power—usually measured in watts, volts, or amperage. Those numbers must be printed on an appliance. If inquiring minds want to know, a very simple math equation will tell you when you are going to reach the limit on a circuit.

It's a good idea to have an electrician survey your home to map and rate your circuits, to upgrade them if need be, and to ensure that your built-in appliances are properly wired. If you hear buzzing or crackling coming from outlets or light switches, don't ignore it. If appliances, extension cords, or switch wall plates are hot to the touch, you have potential problems. Again, contact your electrician.

According to recent statistics from the National Fire Protection Association, an average of 32,000 home fires are caused annually in the U.S. by faulty electrical distribution systems and appliances, taking an average of 220 lives; injuring 950; and causing nearly $674 million in property damage.

Now will you call an electrician?

careening tureen

HOSTS: Polly & Mack Heath
NUMBER OF GUESTS: 12
MENU: Avocado soup, striped sea bass, fava
beans, polenta, strawberry tart

In the mid-seventies, when avocado was all the rage and
making its way into the most fashionable kitchens, I was
invited to a very dignified dinner party at the home of my
good friend, Polly. The guests were seated around the dinner table, eagerly anticipating the first course: chilled
avocado soup.

As an old friend of the hostess, I was lending a hand in the kitchen. We were busily ladling the creamy, green liquid into the tureen, when, suddenly, it slipped off the edge of the counter. Faced with a lake of liquefied avocado creeping its way toward the dining room (due to the unfortunate slant of the floor), I quickly grabbed a cup and began bailing the soup back into the tureen. Polly joined me on the floor, and between giggles and sloshes, we managed to rescue most of the wayward soup and prevent a serious disaster.

Fearing that there might possibly be some unsavory bits from the kitchen floor, Polly and I decided to top each serving with a dollop of chunky salsa. We proudly carried the bowls out to the eager guests.

Polly's recipe was rather novel at the time, and her guests were impressed with such a delicacy. Listening to their "ooh's" and "ahh's," we conscientiously avoided each other's glances so as not to burst out laughing. As the guests praised the potage, only Polly and I knew what the real secret ingredient was: Jubilee floor wax.

CLEANING YOUR HOUSE
WITH KITCHEN INGREDIENTS

Be sure not to use empty commercial cleaning product bottles for your at-home concoctions. You don't want to run the risk of an unwanted chemical reaction or the mistaken use of a bottle of diluted vinegar that is still labeled "Clorox."

For wood floors, mix equal amounts of white distilled vinegar and water. Add fifteen drops of pure peppermint oil and shake to mix. For vinyl and linoleum, add a capful of baby oil to the cleaning water to preserve and polish. For brick and stone tiles, mix one cup white vinegar in one gallon of water, then finish off the job with a rinse of clear water.

A good all-purpose cleaner can be made by mixing a half cup of vinegar and a quarter cup of baking soda into a half gallon of water. Use on bathroom chrome fixtures, windows, bathroom mirrors, etc.

For a homemade air freshener, mix baking soda or vinegar with lemon juice and place in small dishes, which will absorb odors around the house. Having houseplants helps too. Prevent cooking odors by simmering one tablespoon of vinegar in one cup of water on the stove while cooking. To remove fish and onion smells from utensils and cutting boards, wipe them with vinegar and wash in soapy water.

If you must prove your point by eating off your floors, be sure to mind your manners and chew with your mouth closed.

An Odiferous Offering

HOSTS: Kate & Benjamin Pinkerton
NUMBER OF GUESTS: 10
MENU: Foie gras, steak au poivre,
potatoes au gratin, mousse au chocolat

After the birth of my daughter, Paulette, I had managed to defer my hosting duties for nearly two years. However, I had no choice but to shelve my antisocial tendencies and dust off the old *Joy of Cooking* when my husband, Benjamin, was promoted at work. Determined to impress his snooty colleagues at the Institut Pasteur Genopole, Benjamin invited them over for dinner, and I courageously chose a classic French bill of fare for the meal.

Despite my reluctance and the fact that I was woefully out of practice, the evening got underway without a hitch. The guests devoured my first course, a delicate but rich foie gras. Then, as if on cue, Paulette made her entrance. Donned in her favorite velvet party dress with white lace trim, she circled the room to many smiles and coos, finally settling beneath the table at my feet, where she remained, playing contentedly. I was proud of my sometime impulsive tot's impeccable behavior.

Near the end of the main course, a Monsieur Cheval raised his glass to toast me, as the evening's hostess, and Benjamin, as the company's new partner. Our wedding Baccarat clinked festively, and Paulette, as if on cue, emerged from under the table, and dutifully waved *bonne nuit*. My relief at the success of the night blinded me to the site of Paulette's bare bum waddling to bed.

The platter of steak au poivre had nearly made its second way around the table when the aroma of steak was slowly joined, and soon undeniably overtaken, by a much more penetrating odor. Our discreet guests refrained from comment, but their pinched expressions betrayed their growing discomfort. There was no mistaking that smell; every parent of a toddler knows it. Falcon-like, I dove under the table, dodging crossed legs and high heels, to snare Paulette's parting gift to the group: her defiled diaper. Benjamin promptly threw open the window and urged the guests to retreat to the living room. It was time for mousse au chocolat (why hadn't I stuck with the meringue?) and a double Muscat for me.

ODOR MANAGEMENT

It's a safe bet that your home smells, especially if you have a pet, a baby, or if you cook at all. Your household odors may not smell unpleasant to you (and therein lies the danger), but assume that it does to others and take the following preventive actions:

Open a window. Gatherings of people generate more heat than you realize.

Spray your home with undiluted white vinegar or dampen a towel with vinegar and wave it through the air. The vinegar smell evaporates very quickly taking odors with it. Alternatively, place a bowl of vinegar on the counter and let it sit for a few hours.

Dryer sheets can be placed in vents. They will freshen the air as it comes into the room. (This will not work if you have baseboard heating.)

Save citrus peels, cinnamon sticks, and spices that are too old to use. Boil them in a pot with a little hot water.

Put a few drops of your favorite perfume on your lightbulbs.

Put vanilla or fragrant oils on a cotton ball and place it in the bottom of a trashcan or in a drawer.

For those sudden and pungent odors, sulfur does the trick. Light a wooden match in the offending area and the odor will promptly disappear when you extinguish it. A pretty box of matches in the bathroom is always a good idea.

As for personal hygiene, if there's ever a doubt, a hint of perfume or cologne goes a long way!

THE GILDED CAGE

HOSTS: Isabelle & Christopher Claudel
NUMBER OF GUESTS: 200
MENU: Grilled shrimp, broiled snapper with
fresh herbs, skirt steak with chimichurri
sauce, yellow rice and beans, green plantains
with mojo, Cuban-style flan

A few years ago, my favorite nephew was getting married,
and the bride's family was hosting the reception under
tents at their beautiful Miami home. The décor was like
none I'd seen before. The decorators truly outdid themselves, importing exotic flowers from all over the world—
birds of paradise, rare orchids, and Tahitian gardenias.

The tablecloths and napkins were gorgeous, rich-toned raw silk. The caterer had flown in the entire dinner from Cuba, in quantity more than sufficient to feed the two hundred souls in attendance. And, at the center of each table, was a live pair of colorful lovebirds in a gilded cage. To say the least, not one expense was spared.

It was truly an exquisite evening, until something quite unforeseeable happened. Suddenly, out of nowhere, the weather turned. A thunderous rainstorm swept in, the wind violently blowing against the sides and ceiling of the tent. As the powerful gusts assailed the guests, several centerpieces were blown over, allowing a pair of the lovebirds to escape. Freed from their cages, the birds were now having trouble finding their way out of the closed tent. Panicked, they wildly flapped overhead, squawking and fouling the guests and food below. Needless to say, the evening ended quickly after that. No one even got to see the bride and groom cut the cake.

Some people say rain on one's wedding day is a sign of good luck. Alas, this was not the case for my nephew. But while his marriage didn't last, somewhere in Miami, there are two lovebirds happily nesting in freedom.

Bye Bye, Birdie

Lovebirds are known to be escape artists. The bird's technique is to slip its head and shoulders between the bars of its cage, expel its breath, and wriggle forward a little. Then it draws a deep breath, and pops through the bars like a cork.

If your birds discover this route of escape you may want to consider bird diapers to save on cleaning costs. Yes, there are bird diapers that are made of easy breathable fabric that does not inhibit preening, movement, or flight.

Lovebirds acquired their name because of their fondness for sitting in pairs while preening each other's feathers. However, do not be fooled. If you are considering them as pets, beware. Their aggressive chewing habits make them capable of maiming or killing any bird smaller than themselves—which, fortunately, are relatively few. Never house them with finches, canaries, parakeets, or even cockatiels, if you value your other birds.

Lovebirds need a cage that has at least two places to perch, with room to fly from one to the other. A cage with a horizontal measurement of twenty to thirty inches is generally about right. Perches need to be a size that is comfortable for the birds' feet, not too small or too large.

A kitchen precaution: if your bird is to be kept in or near the kitchen, be very careful not to overheat Teflon pans or appliances. When Teflon gets too hot it gives off fumes that are toxic to birds. Teflon-coated irons and other items can also be very dangerous.

THE THRONE

HOSTS: Maria & Anthony West
NUMBER OF GUESTS: 2
MENU: Grilled sirloin steaks,
bleu cheese salad, key lime pie

When Anthony and I were first married, we lived in a vintage highrise in Chicago. The apartment had many problems, but one of its real selling points was the fire escape with a landing just big enough for barbecuing. Access to our "balcony" was gained through a large window in the guest bathroom.

Our first attempts at entertaining were limited to our parents, siblings, and close friends, who would be most tolerant of our inexperience. But then we graduated to a wider circle of guests and invited my uncle and his rather fussy, very proper girlfriend, Judith, for a barbecue. Anthony put the steaks on the grill, rejoined the guests, and then later returned to the fire escape to retrieve the steaks, carefully closing the window behind him to prevent the smoke from blowing into the apartment. When the steaks were done, he opened the window to return to the apartment. You can imagine his surprise as he stepped into the bathroom only to discover Judith sitting on the toilet. Carrying a large platter of meat, he was unable to cover his eyes, nor to entirely hide his amusement while executing an about-face on his heel. With a ceremonious "Excuse me," he returned to the fire escape until she had finished.

No one said a word about the incident, but Anthony and I still laugh about it whenever anyone mentions fire escapes.

Sparking conversation between unfamiliar dinner guests can be more diffi-cult than getting a soufflé to rise. If you're lucky (or if you plan well), you can stack the guest list with one or two ringers who make any conversation flow. If you have a naturally churlish or chilly guest, no one can perform miracles, but the same tactics apply.

Avoid the matchmaking mistake of thinking that because two people are *so* alike they will get on well. Instead, put people together who are interesting, talkative, and have a point of view. The ability to converse outweighs the sim-ilarity quotient.

As host, you can float about the party asking leading questions. It is up to guests to take it from there. Once a conversation starts to bubble, excuse yourself and move on.

Here are a few simple discourse-starter suggestions:

Where did you get that…? (e.g., watch, haircut, delightful escort)

Have you ever…? (e.g., seen *Turandot*, eaten ostrich, pretended to be someone you are not)

Didn't you just get back from…? (e.g., your daughter's wedding, Iceland, Alderson Federal Prison)

How is work going on…? (e.g., your book, your house, your divorce)

What's your take on. . .? (e.g., that new movie, world peace, Tom Cruise)

It is more difficult to silence an overzealous storyteller than to get quieter guests to join a conversation. When the air in the room is being swallowed up by a rambling raconteur, any tactic is acceptable. Suggest the offender assist you in the kitchen, propose a toast, offer a tour of your home, or pop a delectable morsel into his or her mouth.

THe CLOVen HOOFer

HOST: Nell de Becque
NUMBER OF GUESTS: 1
MENU: Roasted chicken, mixed green salad

When I was newly married to my first husband, my mother took ill and ended up in the hospital, leaving my father on the loose for dinner. Ever the dutiful daughter, I invited him for supper. This was fine, except for the fact that I didn't know how to cook. (Prior to my marriage, my mother had called the French Embassy to try to hire one of their chefs to teach me. Oddly enough, they were uninterested in this project, and, while it is hard to imagine the French being rude, they practically hung up on her.)

On this occasion, the butcher was kind enough to direct me to some tender young broilers but failed to tell me to split them before cooking. Needless to say, the tops burned and the bottoms were raw. The dinner was not yet ruined, however, as I had made a nice salad with dressing from a recipe my mother had given me that included lots of chopped shallots.

My father, a famed Broadway composer, hated garlic— probably because he didn't like smelling of it when he went backstage to kiss all the pretty chorus girls. Tonight he sniffed suspiciously at my salad.

"There isn't any garlic in here, is there?"

"Oh, no, no, no," I assured him. "Only shallots, just like Mummy said."

Fortunately for my mother—and unfortunately for my father—I couldn't recognize the difference between the two. And it should be noted that it's a wise child who knows how to deal with a father who kisses chorus girls.

THE STINKING ROSE

In 2004, the International Herb Association declared garlic the Herb of the Year. Folklore attributes garlic with good luck and protection against evil. The smell is said to ward off sorcerers, werewolves, warlocks, and, of course, vampires. King Tut was buried with bulbs of garlic in his tomb, as it was believed to ward off illness and to increase strength and endurance.

An Egyptian papyrus from 1500 B.C. recommends garlic for twenty ailments. Scientists today tell us that the way garlic is prepared appears to affect its healing qualities. When the clove is cut or crushed, an enzyme contained within the plant cells combines with an amino acid. This creates a new compound, called allicin, which has been shown to kill twenty-three types of bacteria, including salmonella and staphylococcus. When garlic is heated, a different compound is formed that researchers believe prevents arteries from clogging and reduces blood pressure and cholesterol levels. The blood-thinning quality of garlic may also be helpful in preventing heart attacks and strokes.

It's hard to cook with garlic without getting some on your hands. After working with garlic, scrub your hands with salt and lemon juice, using cold water. Then rinse off with soapy warm water.

If bad breath is a concern, herbalists recommend chewing fennel seeds or parsley. But the best defense against garlic breath is to have everyone around you indulge as well.

PHANTOM OF
THE OPERA

HOSTS: Christine & Andrew Webb
NUMBER OF GUESTS: 12
MENU: Pumpkin ravioli, chicken marsala,
haricots verts, roasted fennel, poached pears,
vanilla ice cream, biscotti

One evening, as our guests were finishing their pre-dinner
cocktails, a tremendous crash came from the dining room.
We rushed in to find that our enormous French rock-crystal
chandelier was no longer hanging in its accustomed place,
but had fallen into the middle of the dining room table,

already set for fourteen. The cause: my two darling children had let the bath, directly above the dining room, overflow, causing the plaster ceiling to dissolve.

The flower centerpiece was done for but—miracle of miracles—not a single dish was broken. I put some votive lights in the fallen chandelier, which now sparkled magnificently, and voilá, instant ambiance. We dined with our magnificent chandelier as a dramatic centerpiece, and barely noticed the gaping hole in the ceiling.

I hate to think, though, how many heart attacks would have occurred had the chandelier come down with guests seated beneath it. Now that would have been an unforgettable, if unforgivable, evening!

SIMPLE LIGHTING STRATEGIES

Light does more than allow us to see; it enhances our surroundings and affects our mood. Soft, low, or colored lighting can be relaxing or even seductive; bright white light can be stimulating, but can destroy a sense of intimacy. It's important to get the balance right when entertaining.

Consider some of these simple lighting ideas:

Replace existing lightbulbs with colored or low wattage bulbs to tone down a room.

Use white tea lights or votive candles (safely housed within glass holders) in great quantities along window sills, tables, and hallways. But make sure curtains and tablecloths don't catch fire!

Use pillar candles in small groupings down the middle of dining and coffee tables (avoid colored or scented candles).

Place lamps aimed upward on the floor, in corners, or behind furniture to lift focus and create the illusion of space.

If you have a fireplace, use it! If the fireplace is only for show, place candles inside to create a warm glow.

Use large glass bowls as centerpieces. They don't have to be expensive. Fill them with water and float flowers and lit candles in them.

White Christmas tree lights, when carefully strung, can quickly transform your home into a festive party space.

There is nothing like a good power outage, or a fallen chandelier, to rekindle the romance in a candle's glow. Always have plenty of candles on hand, along with a box of kitchen matches. And remember, you don't have to wait until the power goes out or the ceiling falls to enjoy them.

DOG DAYS OF SUMMER

HOSTS: Marguerite & Valentin Wagner
NUMBER OF GUESTS: 20
MENU: Assorted hors d'oeuvres,
rack of lamb, flourless chocolate cake

It was the heyday of the 1980s mergers and acquisitions frenzy. Competition among New York law firms was fierce, as many of the best college graduates, in this climate, had chosen either investment banking or business school. During their summer internships, the students were "wined and dined" so that my husband's firm would be first on their list, should they be offered a job.

One summer, my husband invited twenty of the potential associates to a formal dinner party. Obviously, the intent was for them to be impressed with the lifestyle they would have, should they be one of the lucky ones chosen to join the firm.

I had not entertained since the arrival of our six-month-old cockapoo (a cross between a cocker spaniel and a poodle), named Delia. Delia was a twenty-pound ball of fluff, who looked as if she had walked out of a Walt Disney cartoon. Her whimsical face was crowned with platinum-blonde hair, and her lustrous brown eyes were rimmed with long, black lashes and stand-up eyebrows that were utterly irresistible. She was also rather the handful.

We were very fortunate to know a talented and delightful chef by the name of Diana Hoguet, who would come to our home and prepare a superb gourmet dinner for any parties we hosted. Since Diana was such a gem, I had become rather casual about entertaining. She always brought the same waiters who knew the house, which allowed me to arrive home from work just in time to do the finishing touches before the guests arrived. On the evening of the associates' party, I cheerfully entered the house about 6:45, and as I walked into the kitchen, Diana sheepishly informed me,

"Delia climbed on the table and ate part of the rack of lamb. If you and Valentin don't eat I think we will be okay."

"Don't worry, everything will be fine!" I assured her.

The young lawyers arrived around 7:30, and, as always, we had drinks and hors d'oeuvres in our sizable foyer. Delia, who always believed herself to be human, instantaneously determined that she also wanted a job at the firm. She was to be the paper shredder. Each time a guest was given a drink with a paper napkin, Delia stood on two feet, like a walking bear in a circus, and grabbed the paper napkin away from the guest, shredding it to pieces while shaking her fluffy, blonde head with great self-satisfaction and pride at her accomplishment.

As we entered our dining room for dinner, Delia moseyed in with the rest of the guests, and seemed dismayed that she did not have her own chair. Undeterred, she systematically worked her way around the table to beg for scraps. Valentin, much more proper than I, was mortified and took her into the kitchen. Soon Delia howled and scratched at the door to be released from imprisonment, then escaped by scampering under the waiter's feet, returning to the table.

Thus far, Delia had proved the perfect foil: mischievous but charming. I looked around the table, and everyone appeared to be laughing and having a good time, despite (or perhaps because of) her intrusions. I felt rather pleased with the evening.

For dessert, our guests feasted on chocolate cake, accompanied by a rich chocolate fudge sauce. Stuffed and relaxed, we adjourned from the dining room for coffee and chatted about the associates' summers and school. It was getting rather late when Valentin was summoned to the telephone for an emergency call, which he took in the den.

Delia seized the opportunity: While we were making small talk, she climbed onto the table and devoured the remains of all twenty chocolate desserts. Valentin was kept interminably on the telephone, and finally, at about 11:00, the associates determined that it was time to leave. I walked them to the door to say goodnight. Delia promptly joined us as Valentin covered the telephone with his hand and urgently whispered to me to "walk Delia." But it was too late. No one had ever told us that chocolate was bad for dogs. As the guests bid goodbye, poor Delia's system rebelled against the avalanche of chocolate cake. Directly in front of the door and all our guests, Delia simultaneously threw up and lost control of her bowels, leaving a putrid mess.

I tried to get the attention of the waiters in the kitchen and also motioned to Valentin for help, to no avail. I was left with Delia, the mess, and the summer associates who almost had to jump over this disaster to leave our apartment. In their youthful attempt to be polite they said nothing as I shook their hands and said that I hoped I would see them again.

We were fortunate that Delia, as a puppy, had a constitution sufficiently strong to handle the chocolate, but I was afraid to ask how many of those summer associates joined the firm.

pet precautions

No caring pet pal wants to see Fido or Mittens in a state of discomfort, but not every animal lover is savvy to the perils of certain foods and household items.

The ASPCA recommends that you steer your dog or cat clear of:

Alcoholic beverages
Avocado
Chocolate (all kinds)
Coffee (all kinds)
Fatty foods
Macadamia nuts
Moldy or spoiled foods
Onions and onion powder
Raisins and grapes
Salt
Yeast dough

The holiday season is especially fraught with danger for pets:

Christmas tree water may contain fertilizers, which, if ingested, can upset the stomach. Stagnant tree water can be breeding grounds for bacteria, which can also lead to vomiting, nausea, and diarrhea, if ingested.

Avoid animal exposure to electrical cords. If cords are chewed they could electrocute your pet. Cover up or hide electrical cords and never let your pet chew on them.

Ribbons, tinsel, or rubber bands can become lodged in the intestines and cause intestinal obstruction. This is a very common occurrence in kittens!

Batteries contain corrosives, and if ingested they can cause ulceration to the mouth, tongue, and the rest of the gastrointestinal tract.

Glass ornaments can cause internal laceration when ingested.

Human guests should avoid ingesting these holiday items as well.

VUKUTU

HOSTS: Agatha & Max Weber
NUMBER OF GUESTS: 8
MENU: Chicken salad with melon,
North African couscous

At one time, my husband and I had the great fortune to live on a beautiful 100,000-acre property, called Vukutu, in what is now Zimbabwe. We often ate outside, enjoying the expansive vistas and abundant wildlife. Many a meal was had with antelopes, zebras, and giraffes lolling about nearby. So when Max, then the director of a nationally known art gallery, invited a group of visiting scholars to join us for dinner, I believed our guests might also appreciate the experience of the wild that was our backyard. A table was beautifully set for a simple al fresco meal of chicken salad and melons, perfectly refreshing dishes in the African heat. I instructed Aman, our cook, to put the food out while we took our guests to see the prehistoric cave paintings, walls, and terraces on the property.

By the time we returned from our trek, the guests were quite hungry. As we approached the dining spot, we could make out the figure of Aman, wildly flapping his arms. Only when we got closer could we see that he was trying to rid the table of the last of several Lappet-faced vultures that had invited themselves to our meal. I cringed with the knowledge that vultures, when disturbed, are known to projectile vomit or urinate on themselves. Thankfully, their worst offense was that they had devoured our meal, leaving only a dozen demijohns of Mozambique red wine.

I promptly poured the wine for our guests as Aman tended to the table, and Max, the authentic man of the wild, grabbed his gun and headed off into the bush. We heard shots ring out in the distance, and not too long after, Max returned with a dozen or more small birds roped over his shoulder, as if he did this kind of thing every day.

Flavoring the birds with butter, Aman baked them in our underground earthen ovens. The scholars had quite a story to tell when they got home, and the Vukutu bird became one of our staple dishes.

HOW TO PREPARE A GAME BIRD

Even if you don't plan to actually shoot down your dinner, you may at some time be given fresh game to prepare by those who have. Here's what to do:

First, remove the head, feet, and neck with a sharpened cleaver.

Feathers come out more easily while birds are still warm, so there is no time to waste. Pluck the feathers, a few at a time, in the direction in which they grow. Start at the breast and move toward the neck. Then flip the bird and start plucking away from you toward the tail feathers. After plucking, you may need to singe the bird over a gas flame to burn off any remaining downy feathers or hair.

Birds should be gutted as soon as possible, especially in warm weather. Removing the entrails usually eliminates excess blood, unless the flesh is saturated around the shot. If that is the case, you can soak it in milk or a solution of two quarts of water and one table-spoon baking soda for an hour. Rinse the meat thoroughly after.

Small birds can simply be held up to a light to see any embedded shot. Once the bird is plucked and gutted, examine the bird for any shot or any bits of feather driven in by the shot. Remove this with tweezers or a sharp knife.

If the above makes you squeamish, you can argue that a hunter's task is not complete until the bird is cleaned. But remember, they're armed!

size matters

HOSTS: Mimi & Rodolfo Marcellino
NUMBER OF GUESTS: 4
MENU: Grilled lamb with yogurt and
garam masala marinade, papaya chutney,
basmati rice, puri

A chef friend of ours, who was an associate of a famous—
and famously rotund—chef had invited him to stay with her
for a few days. Knowing our love of cooking, she asked if
we wanted to host a dinner for him one evening. "He likes
Indian food," she announced.

Unfortunately, this cuisine did not frequently appear on
our menu, but we felt we would give it a try. Undaunted, we
rifled through our international cookbooks and consulted
with some student friends from India, who made a few suggestions.

We decided a yogurt and garam masala marinade for grilled lamb would be a good choice, owing to the fact that we had made it years before, and it was not only authentic but tasty to boot. We also prepared an excellent fresh mango chutney and, though inexperienced bakers, made puri, a puffy wheat bread similar to pita.

When the big evening finally arrived, the weather boded well for an al fresco dinner. We set places at a round table in the courtyard. Generally, we can comfortably seat six.

But as we sat down, we realized that our star guest was not only tall but wide. Alas, his bulk would not fit into our chair! Fortunately, he has a delightful sense of humor, so we all had a good laugh at his predicament. We located a sturdy, armless Spanish chair and a plump pillow. With a bit of fancy shuffling, we had a new seating plan, our guest had a new seat, and, much to our relief, despite the chair challenge, the dinner was declared "delish."

Basic Furniture Repair

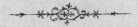

Chair rungs should be checked regularly for looseness and repaired promptly, lest a guest head south for the evening.

If you find a compromised chair, pull the loose chair rung as far out of the socket as you can, apply a generous amount of woodworker's glue into the hole, and pop it back together. As the glue requires pressure to work, tie a rope that runs parallel to the loose rung around the two legs, and then insert a dowel (or a short stick) into the knot and tighten the rope to the desired pressure by turning the dowel. Then slip the dowel behind the chair rung to keep the rope taut and let the glue dry for at least twenty hours before dis-assembling your contraption. Be sure to wipe off the excess glue before it dries or you will have to chip it off.

While you're at it: to remove a water ring, buff the mark lightly with fine-grade steel wool dipped in lemon oil so it doesn't scratch the surface. After you've taken care of the ring, use lemon oil on the whole surface so it all matches—and then use a rag to remove any excess oil.

Wax drippings come off easily if you harden them by laying ice cubes on the wax area. Then use a credit card, spatula-style, to scrape the wax up.

Having said all that, the surest way to prevent wear and tear on your dining room furniture is to eat out!

Bernstein in the Berkshires

HOSTS: Rosa & Gabriel Eisenstein
NUMBER OF GUESTS: 60 plus
MENU: Restuffed lobster, roasted asparagus,
rice pilaf, baked Alaska

My now ex-husband, Gabriel, and I had a wonderful, dis-astrous dinner party for Leonard Bernstein several decades ago at our beautiful mountaintop home in the Berkshires. We had opened our home more than once to the Bernstein entourage for a post- or pre-concert dinner, as Gabriel and I represented a Munich-based company that worked with a "stable" of some of the world's great conductors, including Bernstein himself.

The invitations were sent to about sixty people (probably forty of them to Bernstein regulars: family, friends, and admirers of the family and friends). It was to be rather formal for a Berkshire party—a sit-down dinner under a white tent with red flowers hanging everywhere and an oil lamp on each table. The menu included an entrée of restuffed lobster, which was pretty fancy for us.

In addition to Bernstein's mother, Jennie; his three children; his brother, Burton; and sister, Shirley, Seiji Ozawa had accepted with his mother—so it was shaping up to be a real family occasion. Boston Symphony Orchestra management was also heavily represented, and we had carefully selected a few of our own friends to be part of the not-to-be-missed evening.

Columbia Artists Management president Ronald Wilford, who was coming with his warm and wonderful wife, Sara, called within hours of the party and asked if he might bring some houseguests. I never get stuck on numbers, so I immediately responded, "Of course!" He inquired as to whether I wanted to know the names, and I said it was not really necessary as any friends of his were very welcome.

Pursuing the point, he said, "I think you better know who they are—Slava Rostropovich, Dmitri Shostakovich, and his wife!" My tent out on the Mount Washington lawn would now shelter several of the musical giants of our age—all at one time!

We were all having cocktails under the tent when Bernstein, the last to arrive, pulled up in an open convertible. As Gabriel and I greeted him, he called our attention to some ominous black clouds swiftly moving through the mountain gap toward us. Sure enough, within half an hour, all hell broke loose! The black clouds opened up directly over our tent, and the rain proceeded to fall exactly as it does in the tropics—like a waterfall. The wind picked up and everyone fled to the house.

We convened on the front porch to watch this calamity play itself out. First, the tablecloths and flower arrangements blew off and cartwheeled into the woods. Lamps toppled, and oil spilled on the tables. The tent was shuddering—there had been no time to put up flaps or protect anything.

All eyes, when not on the spectacle unfolding, were on me. (Poor thing! How is she going to deal with all of us and this?) Fortunately, the food was still in the kitchen. My ex, who is known for enjoying the occasional glass of wine, stayed under the tent in the driving and blowing rainstorm with Ozawa and Rostropovich, toasting the elements repeatedly, and singing Russian songs. Now, I don't know about Seiji, but Gabriel does not speak a word of Russian. It didn't seem to matter. We all stood on the porch and watched them intently as if this were a movie.

We used our entire supply of bath towels that night, and the guests dined all over the house. We found lobster shells months later tucked away hither and yon. Champagne and wine glasses were stashed in flowerpots, behind TVs, and in other hard-to-comprehend spots (what were they doing eating in the loft on the beds?).

We consumed a messy dinner in an extraordinarily convivial atmosphere. Rostropovich insisted on helping serve the food and that I eat with him. Lobster was difficult to eat, especially while sitting on Rostropovich's lap! I daresay we had more fun lounging all over the house than we would have at the formal dinner I had planned under the tent.

The next night, as I sat in the box at Tanglewood, still recovering from the night before, Bernstein entered. As he swept past our seats in his theatrical cape, smoking a cigarette, he saw me. He put his hand over his heart and dropped to one knee, as to royalty. I could see heads craning to try to locate the princess to whom he bowed. It was quite a kick for me, and all thanks to "my" storm! That storm had made all the difference and has provided me with memories I surely will always treasure.

OUTDOOR ENTERTAINING TIPS

Mother Nature's sense of humor is often mischievous and ill-timed. Even with the benefit of satellites, radar, and the Internet, one should always be prepared for the possibility of unpredicted extreme temperatures, rain, wind, and pesky bugs when entertaining in the great outdoors.

Have food prepared in advance, but hold off on setting food out until the last moment. Choose a room-temperature menu that does not contain mayonnaise-based sauces or require the use of a knife in case people will eat while standing. Arrange your tables so the food is in the most protected area.

A tablecloth can transform any outdoor table, but it can become a sail in a strong wind. Secure the cloth at each of the four corners, or at intervals on a round table, by either taping or inserting coins into the hem.

Remember, you can never have too much ice. Calculate what you think you'll need and multiply by three. Store the extra ice in the bathtub or in a cool corner of your basement. Always provide your guests with ample cold water in addition to soft drinks and alcoholic beverages.

If bees or wasps are present, avoid red or yellow drinks, which attract these pests, as well as beverage cans, where they can hide for an unpleasant surprise.

You are the leader. Remain calm, regardless of the situation. A sense of humor will usually cure all weather ills. If that fails, you can always try sitting in a guest's lap.

THE PERILS OF PORK

HOST: Robert Meyerbeer
NUMBER OF GUESTS: 50 to 120
MENU: Roasted pork, corn, sausage,
cheese and bread

In my bachelor days, I hosted an annual Pig Party that ultimately turned into nothing less than a series of disasters. The first was held over Fourth of July weekend several years ago. It was a very rustic setting, with a suckling pig roasting over a spit, a keg of beer on a farm wagon, slices of sausage and cheese on big wooden "plates" cut from tree trunks, and 120 cobs of corn—more than enough, I thought, for the 50 invited guests. Problem was, 120 came. They descended like a swarm of locusts. Within two hours, the pig, the corn, the beer, the wine, the sausage, the cheese, and the bread were gone. I think they may have eaten the napkins too! The following morning, I came out to find that one of my (invited) house guests had put up a sign: "Guests of guests cannot bring guests!"

Wise from the first disaster, at Pig Party No. 2, only 50 people were invited, and this time, no guests allowed. I ordered the pig, much larger this time, but when the truck arrived, there was no porker! According to the driver, it was "stolen en route." "Who breaks into a delivery truck to steal dead swine?" I asked. Regardless, what to do? I had to think fast, so I built a gigantic barbecue pit in the adjacent field, bought 50 pork chops, and stuffed and barbecued them with great success.

The following year, now two Pig Parties wiser, I picked up the pigs—two this time—myself. Alas, upon opening the plastic wrap, my nose was met by a most putrid odor. The beasts were rotten! They found their grave in Peconic Bay, where fishermen that year must have wondered about their unusually fat catches. Luckily for me, I was able to phone two friends in Manhattan before they left for the party. They hand delivered two perfectly precooked piglets, right on time.

While the weather gods had smiled on Pig Parties past, No. 4 did not fare so well. It is virtually impossible and absolutely no fun to roast a pig outdoors over a pit in the rain, which soaked us in spite of desperate efforts at rigging a tent. Luckily, the estate I was living on at the time was equipped with two huge ovens, each large enough to handle a pig. Unluckily, in transit from the main house to the cottage, pig juices flowed freely from the frying pans to my car, leaving me for months with a reeking reminder of yet another Pig Party rescue.

At the last Pig Party, which brought an eleven-year tradition to an end, something rather unexpected happened. On this occasion, I bent my no-guests-of-guests rule and allowed a friend to bring a woman friend named Gabriele. Today she is my wife, and that is a very happy ending to the Pig Party stories.

HOW TO ROAST A PIG

Several cooking techniques are available for a pig roast—spit roasting, pit roasting above or in ground, smoking, or oven roasting for those confined to an indoor kitchen. Regardless of method, it is a two-day operation, as the pig must marinate overnight. Place your order with the butcher well in advance of the event, a month if possible, but at least two weeks. When you speak with your butcher, ask for the following:

> Insist he leave on the head, legs, and both ears. (A pig's ear can be coveted as a souvenir.)

> The pig must be cleaned: all hair removed, but skin kept intact.

> The eyes should be removed.

> Ask your butcher to splay the pig—unless you are handy with a hammer and a hatchet. Whoever does the honors, take care not to fully split the snout.

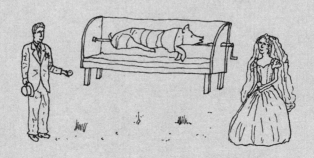

Do not be put off if the butcher informs you that the pig will be frozen. The flavor will not suffer, but do ask that he house the pig until it defrosts at which point you can pick it up.

Fill the pig's cavities with stuffing or your favorite spices, like fresh garlic, rosemary, thyme, sliced onions, ground cumin, lemon, and plenty of salt and pepper. Let the pig rest overnight, in a bathtub filled with ice if possible.

Cooking time can range from four to nine hours depending on the size of the pig. It's ready when the internal temperature registers between 160°F to 170°F. Basting is optional.

Have plenty of side dishes worked into your menu. A roasted pig makes a dramatic presentation with deliciously crispy skin, but ultimately does not yield a lot of meat.

A FINAL NOTE

HOSTS: Eva & Walter Singer
NUMBER OF GUESTS: 35
MENU: Blanquette de veau, wild rice,
Caesar salad

In the early 1960s, my husband, Walter, worked as a music
critic for the *New York Herald Tribune*. This brought him in
touch with many young and gifted musicians. From time to
time we would invite a talented young artist to come to our
apartment on East 10th Street and Tompkins Square and
give a recital, usually as a rehearsal for an upcoming debut

or concert. On these occasions we would invite some of the artist's friends and some of ours, and I would prepare a simple no-knife-necessary buffet.

Vladimir Baku was an exceptionally gifted young cellist, age 19, whom we invited to perform on what turned out to be one of the coldest nights of that or any year. Not since the blizzard of 1937 had there been a more bitterly cold February night for any event, let alone our little musical offering. Tompkins Square was an arctic zone, and parked cars were frozen in place. However, as New Yorkers have little fear of bad weather, the event went on as scheduled, and all thirty-five invitees showed up.

As a woman alone in the kitchen by choice, I was preparing huge pots of *blanquette de veau* (veal stew), overseeing tubs of rice, laundering armloads of lettuce, and slicing bushel-baskets of French bread. As I remember it, the result was one of my better culinary efforts.

At around 8:00, people started arriving, and soon a dozen or more guests were bubbling along in fine party mode. Everything was going swimmingly. Presently, the young guest of honor arrived. With him was his cello, his mother (his coach and a distinguished cellist herself), the wife of his accompanist, and the accompanist's page-turner—a young woman who informed us that the accompanist was having trouble parking his car nearby, and would have to walk several long, cold blocks to the apartment.

Our buzzer buzzed at increasingly rapid intervals as more and more people arrived. At one point an elderly man, quite out of breath, arrived by himself. Walter surmised it was Vladimir's accompanist. The man held out his hand to Walter and gave his name in a heavy German accent.

The man had barely begun to move his lips when he suddenly and utterly collapsed on the floor, falling at Walter's feet inside the threshold of the apartment. As new people continued to arrive, they glanced down at the man on the floor, bewildered, then gingerly stepped over him.

In a moment, the accompanist's wife rushed to his side, knelt down beside him, and fumbled in her purse for heart pills, which she placed in his mouth. In the meantime, Walter called our next-door neighbor, a physician, who, for whatever reason did not appear for some twenty minutes. When he finally did arrive, he examined the man and, turning to Walter and me, pronounced him dead. He then rose to telephone the police and call for an ambulance.

The accompanist's wife went into shock. Our young cellist was dumbstruck and aghast. The page-turner burst into loud sobs. But the cellist's mother, clearly a valiant woman who had survived much suffering, suggested on a note of optimism that while this was a terrible tragedy, her son could at least play some selections of unaccompanied Bach on his cello, which would serve as an instant memorial to the deceased—an idea Vladimir instantly and angrily vetoed. Meanwhile, learning that a corpse was in the room, most of our guests made for the door, once again stepping over the dead man to leave the apartment.

As we waited out the hours for the ambulance to come and remove the body, my twenty-five pounds of *blanquette de veau* also waited. Finally, at around 1:00 in the morning, the remaining nine or ten guests, including the cellist, his mother, the page-turner, and the accompanist's widow, felt there was need for some sustenance. Hunger pangs were stronger than grief, and our musical dinner turned into a wake. Although the body still lay on the floor throughout our meal, people ate heartily, partook of much wine, and a lively conversation began to develop. It was 2:30 in the morning when the ambulance finally arrived to remove the body, and another unforgettable evening at the Singers drew to a close.

The next day, after calling the accompanist's widow with our renewed sympathies, and commiserating by phone with Vladimir, I called several friends to offer a gift of several pounds of *blanquette de veau*. There were only a couple of takers, and Walter and I found that a steady diet of veal stew had its limitations. It would be several decades before I would attempt a *blanquette de veau* again, a smaller one this time. It was not a culinary success.

In Case of Emergency

Not all heart attacks are sudden and intense like in the movies. Most start slowly with mild discomfort or pain. Many people suffering a heart attack may not even be aware that it is happening or may deny it out of fear.

If a guest appears uncomfortable or in pain, be alert for any one or a combination of these "classic symptoms" from the American Heart Association:

> Most heart attacks involve discomfort in the center of the chest that lasts more than a few minutes, or that goes away and comes back. Ask if there is uncomfortable pressure, squeezing, fullness, or pain.

> Find out if there is pain or discomfort in one or both arms, the back, neck, jaw, or stomach.

> Other signs to observe are shortness of breath, cold sweat, nausea, or lightheadedness.

If the above symptoms are present, call 911 immediately. Find out if there is anyone nearby certified in CPR in case the situation worsens before the ambulance arrives. If you can get the person to a hospital quickly by driving, do so without delay. Everyone should take the time to learn CPR at a licensed facility, especially if there is a history of heart disease in your family. Be sure to take refresher classes as recommended.

If you and the stricken guest are lucky, it is simply heartburn, and you can amend your menu for his or her next dining adventure in your home.

THE ANTI-CATASTROPHE PANTRY

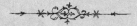

Everyone who entertains has his or her own fallback dishes—things that can be prepared in a pinch, with little or no fuss. The trick is to keep the makings for these dishes on hand at all times. Following is the list of ingredients that I always try to have on hand in case of disaster, or in case guests drop by unexpectedly. Use this list as the basis of your own.

Freezer

Homemade soups
Beef or vegetarian chili
Chicken breast (raw, boneless, and individually wrapped)
Chicken pot pies
Frozen spinach
Extra fancy petit pois (peas)
Unsalted butter
Pesto
Vanilla ice cream
Brownies/cookies

Spice rack

Sea salt
Peppercorns
Dried oregano, thyme, and rosemary
Chili powder
Red pepper flakes

Cabinet

Beef and chicken stock (in can or carton)
Dried pasta
Rice
Olive oil
Vegetable oil
Balsamic vinegar
Good quality tomato sauce in a jar
Chickpeas
Clams (canned)
Smoked salmon (canned)
Bread crumbs
Stone-wheat crackers
Onions
Potatoes

Fridge

Milk
Butter
Eggs
Cream cheese
Mayonnaise
Parmesan cheese
Capers
Carrots
Celery
Fresh parsley

Garlic
Mustard
Hummus
Vinaigrette
Soy sauce
Lemons
White wine

acknowledgments

This book contains entertaining stories written by those who have braved dinner parties throughout the years both as host and guest. My heartfelt gratitude goes to everyone who contributed a story. Not all of the wonderful stories I received could be included in this book—an additional small catastrophe, which I regret; in any case, the names of all contributors have been changed. I am indebted to Anna Jane Hayes for her hard work in collecting the stories and for being the catalyst this book needed. Thank you to Dan Tucker at Sideshow Media for his persistence and patience. Also thank you to Abigail Stokes for her inventive sidebars and to Roderick Mills for his delightful illustrations. And to Andrea Danese and Laura Tam at Harry N. Abrams for helping to bring out the best in our *Disasters*. The book would not have happened without the detailed notes of my daughter, Andrea, and her critical mind. Lastly, a special thank you to my family, whose adventurous palates developed along with my cooking.

For Abrams:
Editors: Andrea Danese and Laura Tam
Production Manager: Jacquie Poirier

Produced by Sideshow Media, LLC

Editor: Dan Tucker
Cover and interior design: Tamar Cohen
Design doctors: Jason Snyder and Matthew Egan

Library of Congress Cataloging-in-Publication Data
Soros, Annaliese.
Dinner party disasters : true stories of culinary catastrophe /
Annaliese Soros with Abigail Stokes ; illustrations by Roderick Mills.
p. cm.
ISBN 13: 978-0-8109-9336-5; ISBN 10: 0-8109-9336-8
1. Dinners and dining. 2. Dinners and dining—Humor. 3. Entertaining.
4. Entertaining—Humor. I. Stokes, Abigail. II. Title.
TX737.S74 2007
642'.40207—dc22
                                    2006036126

Compilation © 2007 Sideshow Media LLC
Introduction and stories © 2007 Annaliese Soros
Sidebars © 2007 Abigail Stokes
Illustrations © 2007 Roderick Mills

Printed and bound in Mexico
10 9 8 7 6 5 4 3 2 1

HNA ▮▮▮▮▮
harry n. abrams, inc.
a subsidiary of La Martinière Groupe
115 West 18th Street
New York, NY 10011
www.hnabooks.com